# The Declaration of Independence

## DAVID & PATRICIA ARMENTROUT

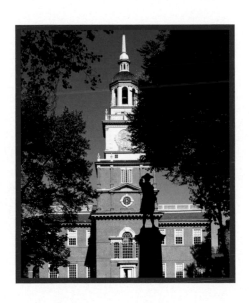

Rourke
Publishing LLC
Vero Beach, Florida 32964

www.rourkepublishing.com

PHOTO CREDITS: Cover and Page 27 © North Wind Picture Archives. Title Page © PhotoDisc, Inc. Page 6 from the Department of the Interior. Page 23 from the Constitution Society. Pages 10, 30 from Images of Political History, Cover Document and Pages 5, 11, Courtesy of the U.S. National Archives and Records Administration. Pages 42, 43 Courtesy of the U.S. National Archives and Records Administration and Earl McDonald. Pages 15, 16 © Getty Images
All other images from the Library of Congress

Title page:  *Independence Hall in Philadelphia, where the Declaration of Independence was signed in 1776*

Editor: Frank Sloan

Cover and page design by Nicola Stratford

Library of Congress Cataloging-in-Publication Data

Armentrout, David, 1962-
  The Declaration of Independence / David and Patricia Armentrout.
     p. cm. -- (Documents that shaped the nation)
  Includes bibliographical references and index.
  ISBN 1-59515-230-X
  1. United States. Declaration of Independence--Juvenile literature. 2. United States--Politics and government--1775-1783--Juvenile literature. I. Armentrout, Patricia, 1960-  II. Title. III. Series: Armentrout, David, 1962-  Documents that shaped the nation.
  E221.A73 2004
  973.3'13--dc22
                            2004014414

Printed in the USA
CG

# TABLE OF CONTENTS

# THE DECLARATION OF INDEPENDENCE

The dictionary defines a document as "a paper that provides information, proof, or support of something else." The Declaration of Independence is one of the most important documents in American history. It describes the reasons and supports the American colonies' demand for independence from Great Britain. It was not the beginning or the end of the American struggle for freedom from Great Britain. The **declaration** is simply a beautifully written statement of the **principles** that justified the American colonies' desire to be free from the nation that controlled them.

Nations are created, dissolved, and changed for many reasons. The United States came into being because colonial settlers did not feel they were treated fairly by the British government. The majority of colonial settlers came from the British Isles, but in America, their rights as British citizens were not clear. The colonists attempted to settle their disagreements with the king and the British government legally, but at last they decided they had no choice but to break away from their mother country and form their own

*This image of the Declaration of Independence is taken from an 1823 engraving. The original document is terribly faded and is exhibited in the Rotunda for the Charters of Freedom at the National Archives in Washington, D.C.*

government. The Declaration of Independence served as notice to Great Britain and the rest of the world that America would not be ruled by **tyranny**. The Declaration of Independence certified the birth of the new nation.

# TAXATION WITHOUT REPRESENTATION

To appreciate just how important the Declaration of Independence was to the American colonies, it is helpful to understand some of the events that led to its creation. Much of the arguing had to do with slavery in America.

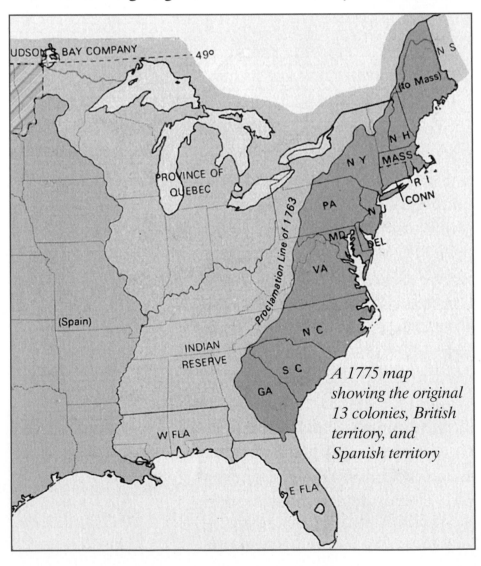

*A 1775 map showing the original 13 colonies, British territory, and Spanish territory*

Great Britain and other European countries colonized North America during the 1600s and 1700s. During much of this period, law and order were left up to the colonists. As the population grew, Great Britain began to exert more control over the colonies. For the most part, the colonists were grateful for the support and protection Great Britain provided. After all, many of the colonists were proud of their British heritage.

The Revolution and the Declaration of Independence came after the colonists began to feel they had lost control over their own affairs. British **Parliament** passed a series of acts, or laws, which the colonists believed were unfair. The colonists were forced to pay taxes and obey British laws, but they had no say or vote in the creation of the laws. This is known as taxation without representation. In other words, colonists had no legal way of changing laws that affected them.

The Charters of Freedom are the founding documents of the United States. They include the Declaration of Independence, the Constitution, and the Bill of Rights.

*Colonists were against the taxes imposed by King George III.*

The French and Indian War ended in 1763, leaving the British in control of 13 colonies. After many years of war, the British had accumulated a large national debt. King George III of England needed money and saw his prospering American colonies as an untapped source of revenue.

Over the next few years, the British Parliament imposed a series of taxes on the colonists. This may have been a reasonable plan; after all, much of the debt had come as a result of British efforts to protect the American colonies. However, each time a new tax was imposed, the colonists became more and more agitated. Colonists opposed the taxes because they had no representatives in Parliament to speak for them.

Colonists opposed taxes, but they were also unhappy about laws that prevented them from creating a colonial paper currency, and laws requiring them to house British soldiers when requested.

# THE SONS OF LIBERTY

British Parliament passed the Sugar Act in 1764, followed by the Stamp Act in 1765. Both were intended to help pay for British debt, which had grown during the French and Indian War. The Acts raised money by taxing the colonists. Many colonists protested by **boycotting**, or refusing to buy, English products. This tactic was very successful because it hit England where it counts—in the pocketbook.

Some colonists took the protest a step further. They created a secret network of protesters who called themselves the Sons of Liberty. Members of the group threatened and intimidated the king's tax collectors. Again, the efforts were successful. Many of the tax collectors resigned, making it almost impossible to collect the taxes.

*Members of the Sons of Liberty are shown harassing a tax collector.*

*The Stamp Act forced colonists to buy and place stamps on items such as newspapers. This article states that this paper will no longer be printed unless the Stamp Act is repealed.*

Some British officials believed troops should be sent to force the colonists to obey the tax laws. In 1766, however, Parliament decided to **repeal** the Stamp Act. Colonists responded by lifting their boycott of British products.

Parliament's change of heart did not mean they were

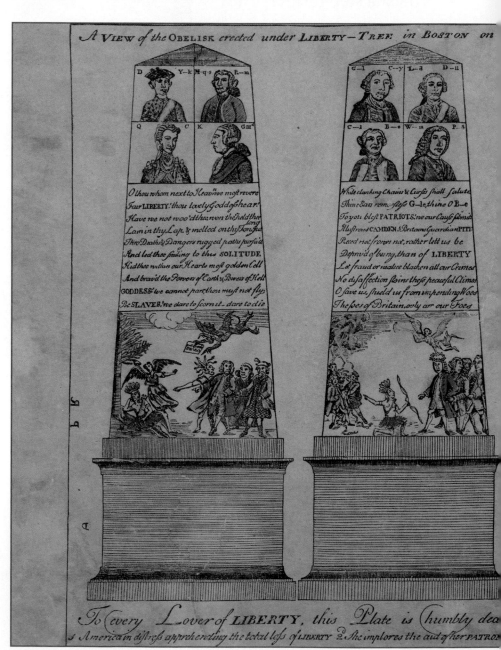

*Paul Revere designed this four-sided pillar, called an obelisk, to celebrate the repeal of the Stamp Act.*

loosening their grip on the colonies. In fact, the same day they repealed the Stamp Act, they passed the Declaratory Act. This act basically stated that Parliament had complete authority to make, change, and enforce any and all laws over the colonies at will.

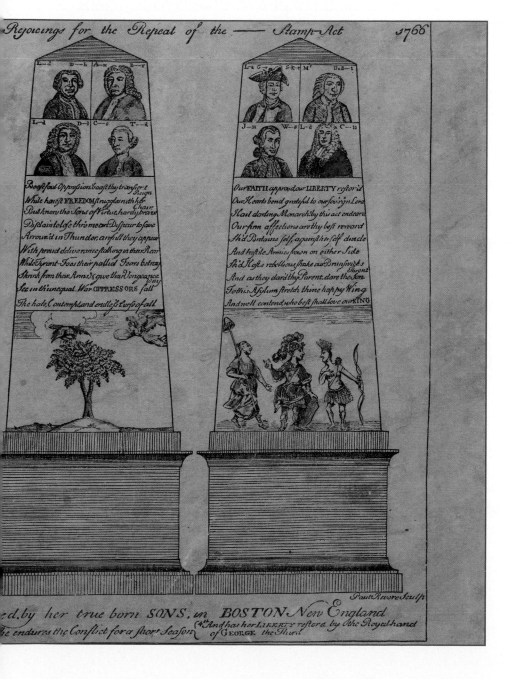

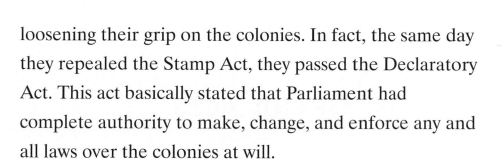

# THE TOWNSHEND ACTS

Parliament's next big attempt to tax the colonies came in the form of the Townshend Acts of 1767. The Townshend Acts taxed a variety of products such as paper, paint, and tea. Again, the colonists responded by boycotting British goods.

In 1768, a famous **patriot** named Samuel Adams wrote a paper criticizing Parliament's actions. He argued that the colonies should not be taxed without representation. Adams called for the colonists to stand together and oppose the unfair taxes. The Massachusetts House of Representatives in Boston approved his paper. The paper was supported by most of the colonies. In response, British troops were sent to Boston, and the Massachusetts Legislature was dissolved.

In 1769, Virginia's House of Burgesses passed resolutions supporting Massachusetts. Virginia's royal governor immediately dissolved Virginia's legislature, just as had been done in Massachusetts.

*American patriot and politician Samuel Adams*

# THE BOSTON MASSACRE

By 1770, tensions between Great Britain and the American colonies had reached a dangerous level. On March 5, a crowd of unhappy colonists gathered around a group of British soldiers in Boston. Words were exchanged and tensions mounted. The nervous soldiers opened fire, killing five colonists. This event became known as the Boston Massacre.

Angry colonists protested the killings, and the soldiers were put on trial for murder.

Patriot John Adams, who believed the soldiers had the right to a fair trial, defended the soldiers in court. Six of the soldiers were cleared of all charges. Two others were found guilty of a lesser charge. As was common practice during the period, the two soldiers were **branded** on the hand and then released.

A period of calm followed the Boston Massacre. Parliament watered down the Townshend Acts by reducing most of the taxes, but trust between the colonies and their mother country had been all but lost. Although tensions were high, few serious events occurred until 1773.

*Soldiers open fire on colonists in this painting of the Boston Massacre.*

# THE BOSTON TEA PARTY

Many colonists still supported a boycott against British products. This included tea that was imported into the colonies by the British East India Company.

Instead, the colonists were buying tea from Holland. In 1773, British Parliament passed the Tea Act, which allowed the British East India Company to sell directly to colonists, bypassing colonial **merchants**.

Although this made British tea cheaper, many colonists felt it was unfair to colonial merchants. On December 16, members of the Sons of Liberty dressed as Native Americans and boarded British ships loaded with tea. The men dumped 45 tons of British tea into the harbor and then quietly returned to their homes.

*The Boston Tea Party took place in 1773.*

# THE INTOLERABLE ACTS

The British response to the illegal dumping of tea was swift. Aiming to punish their misbehaving colonies, Parliament passed several laws known together as the Intolerable Acts, or the Coercive Acts. One act closed Boston's port by making it illegal to load or unload ships until the city paid for the tea that was destroyed. A second act insured that the English Crown would have control over the election of colonial officials and banned unauthorized town meetings.

Several other acts were also designed to take a heavy hand against the colonies. The Intolerable Acts did have one important effect on the colonies. They united the colonists as never before. The colonies agreed they needed to organize their protest. They decided to form a congress to discuss the issues.

*British Prime Minister Lord North proposed the Intolerable Acts.*

*Engraved for Murray's History of the American War.*

*Pollard sculp.*

# FREDERICK lord NORTH.

*Printed for T. Robson, Newcastle, upon Tyne.*

# THE FIRST CONTINENTAL CONGRESS

In 1774, 12 of the 13 colonies sent **delegates** to a meeting of the First Continental Congress. Fifty-six

delegates represented all but Georgia in this historic first meeting. Among the leaders at the meeting were Patrick Henry and George Washington of Virginia, and Samuel Adams and John Adams of Massachusetts. The delegates agreed to encourage a complete boycott of British products and to protest unfair measures taken by British Parliament.

Groups of colonists, called **militia**, armed themselves for possible military action against the British. Massachusetts went a step further and created special units of militia known as Minutemen. The Minutemen could be called to arms at a "minute's notice." Other colonies also formed their own Minutemen militias.

*This patch was worn by some members of the colonial militia.*

*Patrick Henry supported American independence and spoke against the Stamp Act.*

# THE BATTLES OF LEXINGTON AND CONCORD

On April 19, 1775, British troops en route from Boston to Concord encountered a company of Minutemen at Lexington, Massachusetts. Someone panicked and fired a shot. Then the British and the Minutemen shot at one another. Several militiamen were killed.

The famous "Midnight Ride of Paul Revere" took place on April 18 and 19, 1775. At great risk to himself, patriot Paul Revere rode through the countryside warning colonists that the British were coming.

*The Battle of Lexington was the first battle of the Revolutionary War.*

The British troops, searching for a stash of colonial gunpowder near Concord, continued on their way. After finding and confiscating a small amount of gunpowder and arms, the troops began their return trip to Boston. However, news of the incident had spread quickly. On their way back to Boston, members of the Massachusetts militia ambushed the British soldiers, causing hundreds of casualties.

*Paul Revere warned John Hancock and Samuel Adams that British troops were coming to arrest them.*

# THE SECOND
# CONTINENTAL CONGRESS

By the time the Second Continental Congress was called to order on May 10, 1775, the American Revolution had already begun. Many of the delegates had represented their colonies at the First Continental Congress. There were also some notable additions such as Thomas Jefferson of Virginia, Benjamin Franklin of Pennsylvania, and John Hancock of Massachusetts. The colonial representatives elected John Hancock president of the Second Continental Congress.

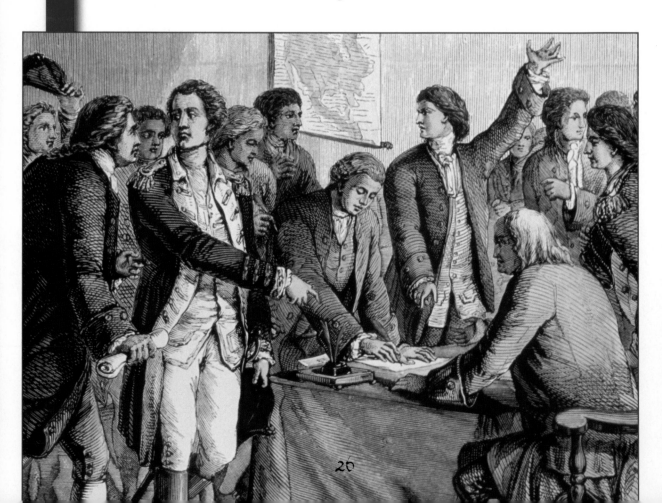

The historic meeting of the Second Continental Congress was at Independence Hall in Philadelphia. The group discussed what to do about the fighting at Lexington and Concord. Some members of the Congress wanted to declare independence immediately. Others wanted to avoid war with their mother country. Congress agreed to a

*John Hancock is known for his recognizable signature on the Declaration of Independence as well as his important role in American history.*

two-step plan. They would make one last effort for a peaceful solution but at the same time prepare the colonies for an all out war.

*The colonies sent delegates to represent them at the meeting of the Second Continental Congress.*

*John Adams was a delegate to the First and Second Continental Congresses and the second president of the United States from 1797 to 1801.*

On June 10, 1775, John Adams, a leading delegate from Massachusetts, suggested that the Congress take command of the colonial forces in New England. Adams also proposed that George Washington, a delegate from Virginia, be named as the commander-in-chief of the new Continental army. Washington accepted the assignment on June 17.

After years of heading the Virginia militia and later commanding the Continental army, Washington was able to go home to Mount Vernon. It wasn't until 1789, six years after the war was officially over, that George Washington became the first president of the United States.

*John Dickinson wrote the Olive Branch Petition. It was America's final attempt at a peaceful solution to the Revolution.*

John Dickinson, a delegate from Pennsylvania, was given the task of writing a document titled the Olive Branch Petition. This document was an appeal to King George III of England to recognize the rights of the colonists. In return, the colonists would pledge their loyalty to the British crown. The effort was in vain, as the king refused to even read the petition.

The king was **defiant**. He proclaimed the protesters **rebels** and lawbreakers. Any colonists who stood against British authority risked harsh penalties.

Congress increased its war preparation efforts by stockpiling supplies, creating an American navy, and enlisting support from foreign nations such as France. The British were also planning for war. The decision had been made. The time for talking and debating was over. Control for the colonies would have to be determined on the battlefield.

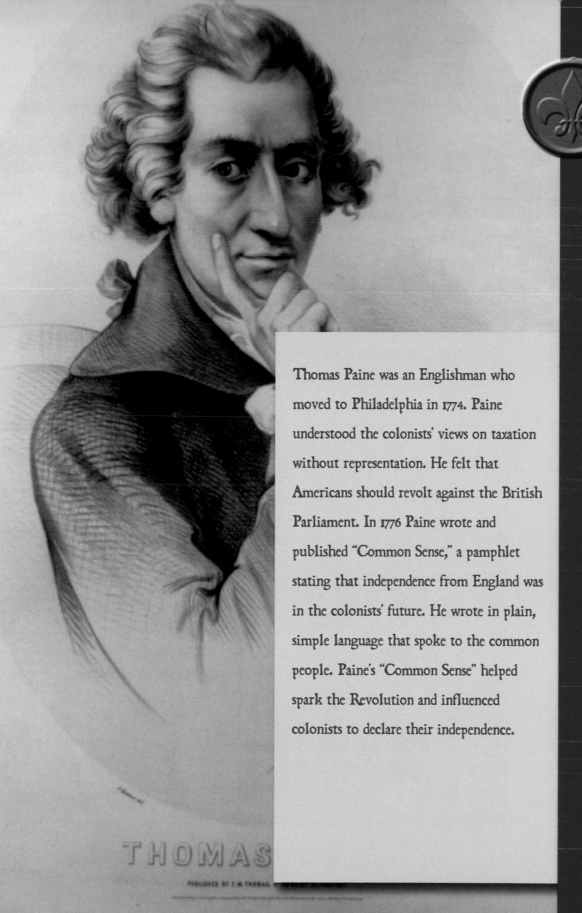

Thomas Paine was an Englishman who moved to Philadelphia in 1774. Paine understood the colonists' views on taxation without representation. He felt that Americans should revolt against the British Parliament. In 1776 Paine wrote and published "Common Sense," a pamphlet stating that independence from England was in the colonists' future. He wrote in plain, simple language that spoke to the common people. Paine's "Common Sense" helped spark the Revolution and influenced colonists to declare their independence.

THOMAS

# THE DECLARATION COMMITTEE

On June 11, 1776, the Second Continental Congress formed a **committee** to draft one of the most important documents in American history. The document would be a declaration explaining the reasons the American colonies wanted independence from Great Britain. Congress wanted the world to know why such drastic action against Great Britain had become necessary.

*The Declaration Committee was given the task of writing the Declaration of Independence.*

The committee consisted of five men: John Adams, Benjamin Franklin, Thomas Jefferson, Roger Sherman, and Robert Livingston. The committee agreed that the job of writing the first draft of the document would best be completed by one man. Since Thomas Jefferson had already earned a reputation for literary craftsmanship, he was asked to put his skill to work writing the declaration.

Thomas Jefferson (1743-1826) served as the first secretary of state, vice president to John Adams, and two terms as our third president. By his own instruction, though, he wanted to be remembered by "the following inscription, and not a word more. Here was buried Thomas Jefferson author of the Declaration of American Independence, of the Statute of Virginia for religious freedom, and Father of the University of Virginia."

Thomas Jefferson recognized the importance of the job he had accepted. Looking for a quiet place in which to devote himself to writing, he rented a couple of rooms in a small house on the outskirts of Philadelphia. Jefferson consulted the other members of the committee. However, credit for writing the document goes almost exclusively to Jefferson. He completed the first draft in less than three weeks.

# THE OLD EPHRATA PRINTING PRESS.

The Old EphrataPrintingPress, on which the Declaration of Independence was printed, and the Original House, No. 702 Market Street, in which it was actually written by **THOS. JEFFERSON.**

*A newspaper article with drawings of the house (right) where Thomas Jefferson drafted the Declaration of Independence, and a printing press (left) on which the Declaration was printed after the War.*

With a few minor changes, the committee presented the Declaration of Independence to the Second Continental Congress. Congress made a few more changes before approving the document on July 4, 1776, a date that came to be known as Independence Day. Formal signing of the Declaration of Independence by Congress took place on August 2, 1776. Copies of the document were printed and sent throughout the colonies.

The Declaration House is part of the Independence National Historical Park in Philadelphia. Philadelphia Bricklayer Jacob Graff, Jr. built the house in 1775. The following year Thomas Jefferson, seeking a quiet place to write, rented two rooms on the second floor. It was there that Jefferson drafted the Declaration of Independence. The Declaration (Graff) House was reconstructed in 1975. It now displays period furnishings and reproductions of the swivel chair and the lap desk used by Jefferson.

The Declaration of Independence changed the direction of the dispute with Great Britain. The colonists would no longer be satisfied with an agreement for fair treatment from their mother country. They wanted complete control of their own future. They wanted freedom.

John Dunlap was a Philadelphia printer who produced the first printed text of the Declaration of Independence. The printing began late on July 4, 1776 and continued into the next day. It is not certain how many prints were made, but only 25 original copies remain.

*Franklin, Adams, and Jefferson review a draft of the Declaration of Independence.*

# THE WAR OF INDEPENDENCE IS OVER

The War of Independence was costly. Thousands of American colonists died or were injured fighting for freedom. Many others died from disease. The colonists were not alone in their suffering. France, the first to side with the Americans, sent troops to fight alongside colonial soldiers. The colonists were also supported by Spain and Holland. The British and their Native American **allies**, as well as loyalists in America and Canada, also suffered dearly.

The Treaty of Paris in 1783 finally brought the Revolutionary War to a close. Great Britain agreed to cease hostile action and to recognize the United States as a sovereign nation.

The Declaration of Independence served its purpose very well. Many colonists, who had not yet made up their minds about a war with Great Britain, were inspired by the document. It united the colonies in a way that had never been done before.

*George Washington and other officers ride through New York City after the Treaty of Paris.*

# THE SIGNERS OF THE DECLARATION OF INDEPENDENCE

Congress formally signed the Declaration of Independence on August 2, 1776. John Hancock, the President of Congress, was the first to sign. His signature, in the center just below the text, is the largest and boldest. The other delegates signed in order of the geographic location of the state they represented. Delegates from New Hampshire,

*Delegates leave the Pennsylvania State House, now called Independence Hall, after signing the Declaration of Independence.*

the northernmost state, signed first, and delegates from Georgia, the southernmost state, signed last. A number of the delegates were not present on August 2, and they signed the document later. In all, 56 delegates eventually put their signatures on the Declaration of Independence.

John Adams and Thomas Jefferson were the only two signers of the Declaration of Independence who went on to become presidents. In a strange twist of fate, they both died on the same day, Independence Day, July 4, 1826.

*John Hancock proudly displays his signature on the Declaration of Independence.*

# PRESERVING THE DECLARATION OF INDEPENDENCE

During the revolution, the Declaration of Independence was moved about as the Continental Congress was forced to relocate as a matter of security. Since then, the document has been moved numerous times, but eventually found a permanent home at the National Archives in Washington, D.C.

At the National Archives in Washington, D.C., more than 5,000 people stand in line daily waiting to view the Declaration of Independence.

*The Rotunda, at the National Archives, where the Charters of Freedom are on public display.*

The Declaration of Independence was printed on **parchment** and during its early years was rolled up for storage. Each time it was rolled or unrolled for use, the document was exposed to damage. Years of use and abuse, sunlight, and improper storage took a toll on the document and eventually it began to fade. Periodically, efforts have been made to restore and preserve the document for future generations.

*A conservator carefully examines and cleans a document.*

In July of 2001, the Declaration of Independence was removed from public display as part of a major restoration project. Scientists microscopically examined every portion of the parchment. Small flakes of loose ink and parchment were painstakingly reattached. The document was cleaned and housed in a specially designed case. The new case is filled with argon gas, which will protect the document from environmental damage. A narrow light beam travels through small portholes in the side of the case to monitor the atmosphere inside.

The restoration project will preserve this most important American document for many years to come. The new display at the National Archives in Washington, D.C. opened to the public in September of 2003.

# TIME LINE

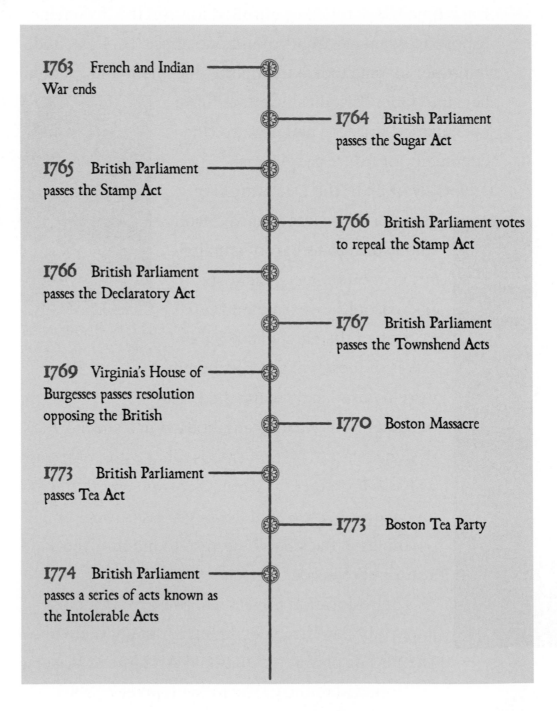

**1763** French and Indian War ends

**1764** British Parliament passes the Sugar Act

**1765** British Parliament passes the Stamp Act

**1766** British Parliament votes to repeal the Stamp Act

**1766** British Parliament passes the Declaratory Act

**1767** British Parliament passes the Townshend Acts

**1769** Virginia's House of Burgesses passes resolution opposing the British

**1770** Boston Massacre

**1773** British Parliament passes Tea Act

**1773** Boston Tea Party

**1774** British Parliament passes a series of acts known as the Intolerable Acts

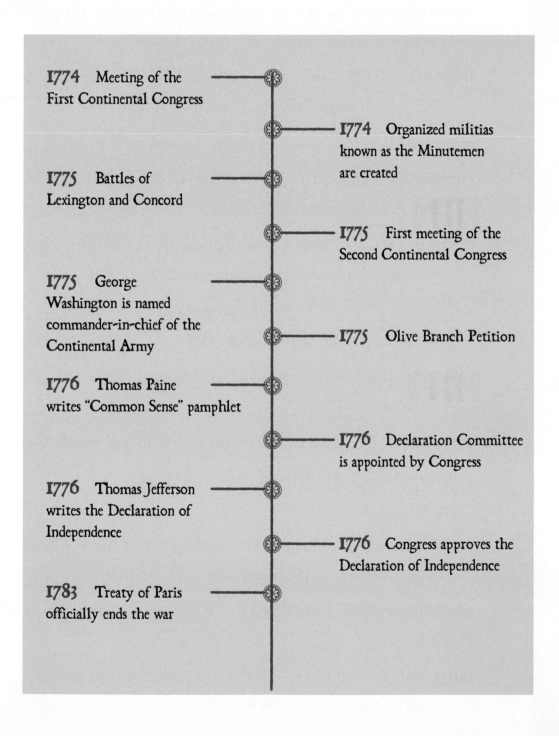

**1774** Meeting of the First Continental Congress

**1774** Organized militias known as the Minutemen are created

**1775** Battles of Lexington and Concord

**1775** First meeting of the Second Continental Congress

**1775** George Washington is named commander-in-chief of the Continental Army

**1775** Olive Branch Petition

**1776** Thomas Paine writes "Common Sense" pamphlet

**1776** Declaration Committee is appointed by Congress

**1776** Thomas Jefferson writes the Declaration of Independence

**1776** Congress approves the Declaration of Independence

**1783** Treaty of Paris officially ends the war

# GLOSSARY

**allies** (AL eyez) — people or countries that give support to another

**boycotting** (BOY kot ing) — refusing to buy something or take part in something as a way of protest

**branded** (BRAND ed) — a mark burned on the skin

**committee** (kuh MIT ee) — a group of people chosen to discuss things and make decisions for a larger group

**declaration** (dek luh RAY shuhn) — the act of announcing something or the announcement made

**defiant** (di FYE uhnt) — standing up to someone or an organization and refusing to obey

**delegates** (DEL uh gates) — those who represent others at a meeting

**merchants** (MUR chuhnts) — people who sell goods for profit

**militia** (muh LISH uh) — a group of citizens trained to fight in a time of emergency

**parchment** (PARCH muhnt) — heavy paper like material made from animal skin and used for writing

**parliament** (PAR luh muhnt) — a group of people elected to make laws

**patriot** (PAY tree uht) — someone who loves his or her country and is prepared to fight for it

**principles** (PRIN suh puhlz) — basic truths, laws, or beliefs

**rebels** (REB ulz) — people who fight against a government

**repeal** (ri PEEL) — to do away with

**tyranny** (TIHR uh nee) — ruling other people in an unjust or
  cruel way

## FURTHER READING

Fink, Sam. *The Declaration of Independence.*
  Scholastic, Inc. 2002.
Freedman, Russell. *Give Me Liberty: The Story of the Declaration
  of Independence.* Holiday House, 2002.
Jones, Veda Boyd. *Thomas Jefferson: Author of the Declaration
  of Independence.* Chelsea House Publishing, 2000.
Murray, Stuart. *American Revolution.* DK Publishing, 2002.

## WEBSITES TO VISIT

http://www.americanrevwar.homestead.com/

http://www.loc.gov/exhibits/declara/

http://www.ushistory.org/declaration/

http://www.congressforkids.net/Independence_declaration_1.htm

## ABOUT THE AUTHORS

David and Patricia Armentrout have written many nonfiction
books for young readers. They have had several books published
for primary school reading. The Armentrouts live in Cincinnati,
Ohio, with their two children.

# INDEX